The Country Kitchen
SPICES
Barbara Beckett

The Country Kitchen

SPICES

Barbara Beckett

Bloomsbury Books
London

Front and back of jacket: Spices are not just for curries-use them to flavour cakes, soups and fruit. From the left, spiced grapes (p. 17), ginger cake (p. 21) pumpkin soup (p. 14), peanut sauce for satay (p. 45), Thai curry paste (p. 31), chicken kebabs with tandoori marinade (p. 44) and a plate of colourful spices.

Front and back endpapers: An old-fashioned country kitchen with the preparation for a spicy fruit cake in the foreground. The wood burning stove is wonderful for long, slow cooking.

Page 2: Serve pitta bread with this spicy pumpkin dip. I think butternut pumpkins have the finest taste and texture of all the pumpkin family.

 COOK'S NOTES: Standard spoon measurements are used in all recipes.
All spoon measurements are level.
1 tablespoon = 15 ml spoon
1 teaspoon = 5 ml spoon

As the imperial and metric equivalents are not exact, follow either one or other system of measurement.
All ovens should be preheated to the specified temperature. Fresh herbs are used unless otherwise stated. If they are unavailable, use half the quantity of dried herbs. Use freshly ground black pepper whenever pepper is used; add salt and pepper to taste. Flour, unless stated otherwise, means plain flour. Fresh root ginger is used unless otherwise stated. Use fresh chillies or half the quantity of dried. I use cold-pressed virgin olive boil but any type may be used. Vinegar is white wine fermented vinegar.

Published by Harlaxton Publishing Ltd
2 Avenue Road, Grantham, Lincolnshire, NG31 6TA, United Kingdom.
A Member of the Weldon International Group of Companies.

First published in 1992.

© Copyright Harlaxton Publishing Ltd
© Copyright design Harlaxton Publishing Ltd

This edition published in 1993 by
Bloomsbury Books
an imprint of
The Godfrey Cave Group
42 Bloomsbury Street, London. WC1B 3QJ
under license from Harlaxton Publishing Ltd.

Publishing Manager: Robin Burgess
Project Coordinator: Barbara Beckett
Designer: Barbara Beckett
Illustrator: Amanda McPaul
Photographer: Ray Jarratt
Editor in United Kingdom: Alison Leach
Typeset in United Kingdom: Seller's, Grantham
Produced in Singapore by Imago

British Library Cataloguing-in-Publication data.
A catalogue record for this book is available from the British Library.
Title: Country Crafts Series: Spices
ISBN:1 85471 106 7

CONTENTS

INTRODUCTION

SPICES and condiments have been used to flavour food for thousands of years. Each national cuisine arrived at its own mixture, or was influenced by a neighbouring country (or a newly discovered one). Spices have been used for many purposes. In cooking, they stimulate the gastric juices and enhance the flavour of food. Before refrigeration, they helped preserve food. And in medicine, they have been used to protect and cure. Many spices were thought to possess either religious or magical properties.

Spices are the fried aromatic parts of plants, such as buds, bark, fruit, pods, roots, berries, seeds, or even flower stigmas. Initially, they were mostly grown in a few tropical countries such as Sri Lanka (Ceylon), the West Indies and Indonesia. As demand grew in Europe, routes were opened up to bring spices to the colder countries from the far-flung colonies. Ships carried spices halfway round the world, and Arabs brought them by caravan through the Middle East from India and China. As countries struggled to gain a monopoly over particular spices, many wars were fought over lucrative rights to the spice trade. Nowadays, most spices can be grown in any tropical country and, as they become freely available,

they are increasingly experimented with and introduced to local cuisine's everywhere.

As interesting and tasty as spices may be, they are only one element of a well-cooked dish. Be careful not to overdo a flavouring, but to harmonise the flavours to complement the basic ingredient, whether fish, rice, chicken, beef or vegetables. Different cooking methods, such as roasting, stewing or frying, will vary the flavour of the same ingredients, as will the type of oil and the quality of the water or wine used. Follow these recipes carefully before beginning your own experiments in spice cooking.

Bear in mind, also, that spices will not disguise ingredients that taste bad, and that quality meat and vegetables will always taste better if cooked correctly. It is better to have less of a fine ingredient than a large quantity of an inferior one.

I hope that you enjoy cooking with these recipes. Most of them are hearty country fare, many are economical as well, but I could not resist the occasional festive dish. After all, cooking and eating celebrate life–and what is better than eating and drinking good food and wine around a table with family and friends?

A rich spicy ginger cake that will last for weeks in a cake tin, if you are able to resist it for that long.

7

ALLSPICE

ALLSPICE is the dried berry of the evergreen tree *pimenta officinalis*. Sometimes it is known as pimento. It came originally from Jamaica but is now grown in many tropical countries. Its taste resembles a mixture of cloves, cinnamon and nutmeg. It is very popular in Middle Eastern cooking.

Its main use is in pickling vegetables and meats. Ground, it can be used to flavour spiced cakes and biscuits. Keep some berries in a pepper mill and grind whenever you need the fresh taste of cloves, cinnamon or nutmeg.

Stuffed Aubergine (Eggplant)

This aubergine, stuffed with a spicy meat mixture, can be eaten as a vegetable or as a meal in itself.

3	medium sized aubergine
1	tablespoon salt
	Oil
FOR THE STUFFING	
1	tablespoon oil
45 g	(1 1/2 oz) onion, chopped
3	garlic cloves, crushed
315 g	(10 oz) minced beef
315 g	(10 oz) tomatoes, finely chopped
1	teaspoon salt
1	teaspoon pepper
1 1/2	tablespoons ground allspice
1	tablespoon sultanas
30 g	(1 oz) parsley, finely chopped

Cut the aubergines in half and sprinkle with the salt. Leave to drain for an hour. Wash and dry the aubergines and brush them with oil. Transfer to an ovenproof dish, and cook for 1 hour in a preheated oven (200°C; 400°F; gas 6). In the meantime, make the stuffing. Heat the oil in a pan and gently cook the onions until they are soft and translucent. Add the beef and garlic and cook stirring for several minutes. Put in the tomatoes, spices and sultanas and simmer, for 30 minutes. Add the parsley at the last minute.

Remove the aubergines from the oven. Press the pulp down and cover the aubergines with the meat mixture, pressing the mixture down into the eggplant shells. Put back into the oven and cook for a further 15 minutes. Serves 6.

VARIATION: Replace the minced beef with 315g (10 oz) of cooked rice for a vegetarian meal.

Spiced Turkey

A spicy, sweet turkey to cook as a change from the usual recipes. A large chicken will taste wonderful cooked this way, too.

5 kg	(10 lb) turkey
2	lemons
FOR THE STUFFING	
1	tablespoon oil
1 kg	(2 lb) mixed minced veal and pork
75 g	(2 1/2 oz) flaked almonds
60 g	(2 oz) walnut halves
75 g	(2 1/2 oz) pistachio nuts, shelled
500 g	(1 lb) long-grain rice
155 g	(5 oz) sultanas
1	tablespoon ground allspice
1	tablespoon ground cinnamon
FOR THE BASTING MIXTURE	
3	tablespoons oil
1	teaspoon ground allspice
1	teaspoon ground cinnamon

Cut lemons in half and rub all over the outside and inside of the turkey.

Make the stuffing by browning the meat in a pan with the oil, stirring constantly. Add the

Stuffed aubergines are a popular dish in the Middle East. The same stuffing goes well with tomatoes and peppers.

nuts, rice, sultanas and spices and keep stirring until they are well mixed and warm. Stuff the turkey with the mixture and sew it up, leaving room for the rice to expand.

Mix together the basting ingredients and paint all over and under the skin, gently prising open on the breast and thighs. Put into a large roasting tin with 2.5cm (1 in.) of water. Put the turkey into a preheated oven (220°C;

425°F; gas 7). Reduce to 160°C (325°F; gas 3) after 30 minutes. Cook for a further 25 minutes per 500 g (1 lb). Baste with allspice mixture three times. Serves 10.

VARIATION: Soak the sultanas in 125 ml (4 fl oz) brandy for an hour before cooking. Add the leftover brandy to the basting mixture.

Spiced Beef

Serve this meat loaf with a rich gravy and mashed potatoes, or cold with a salad and a fresh tomato sauce.

1.5 kg	(3 lb) lean minced beef
3	bacon rashers, chopped
1	tablespoon chopped thyme
1	tablespoon ground allspice
1	teaspoon salt
1	teaspoon pepper
3	garlic cloves, chopped
125 ml	(4 fl oz) Port
1	tablespoon lemon juice
2	eggs
6	bay leaves

Put all ingredients except the bay leaves into a large bowl and mix well, then place into a large greased loaf tin or two small ones.

Smooth the surface and decorate with bay leaves. Stand the tin in a baking tin, one-third filled with water. Cover with foil. Put into a pre-heated oven (180°C; 350°F; gas 4) for 1 1/2 hours or until cooked. Remove foil for the last 30 minutes to brown the surface. Serves 6-8.

ANISEED (ANISE)

ANISEED (anise seeds) is used in cooking to flavour breads and cakes and fruit tarts. The other important use is to flavour liqueurs and cordials. Most Mediterranean countries have an alcoholic drink flavoured with anise, such as Pernod, Ouzo, arak and Sambucca. These liqueurs are often used to enhance seafood and chicken dishes.

A spicy pick-me-up on a lazy afternoon, anise liqueur served with spice cake.

Anise Liqueur

This is a delicious aperitif or after dinner drink, served chilled with ice. Spiced liqueurs used to be drunk as medicine and a general sort of pick-me-up.

1 litre   (1 3/4 pints) vodka
45 g   (1 1/2 oz) aniseed, crushed
1/2   teaspoon ground cinnamon
2   tablespoons ground coriander
440 g   (14 oz) caster sugar

Put vodka and spices into a large jar. Dissolve the sugar in 125 ml (4 fl oz) of water in a pan, pour it over the vodka and mix well. Leave to stand in a dark place for a month, shaking the jar once or twice a week. Strain and bottle.

CARAWAY

CARAWAY is native to most of Europe and Russia. We know the dried seeds were used by the Romans and that the fresh leaves were served as a garnish. Today, caraway is used extensively to flavour cabbage dishes, cheeses and cheesecakes, as well as bread and hearty meat dishes.

Potato Bread

This bread is surprisingly light and full of flavour. Delicious to eat for lunch while it is still warm, spread with herb butter.

1 kg   (2 lb) potatoes
125 ml   (4 fl oz) hot milk
15 g   (1/2 oz) dried yeast
1.5 kg   (3 lb) flour
1   teaspoon salt
2   tablespoons aniseed

Cook the potatoes, peel them and mash with the hot milk over the heat until you have a batter. Dissolve the yeast in 75 ml (2 1/2 fl oz) of water and leave to stand until frothy. When the batter has reached room temperature mix in the yeast, flour, salt and 1 tablespoon aniseed. Knead well and leave to rise in a warm place for 4 hours. Put into greased baking tins, sprinkle remaining aniseed on the top, and cook in a preheated oven (190°C; 375°F; gas 5) for 50 minutes or until cooked.

Spicy Pumpkin Dip

Serve this pumpkin dish hot as a vegetable, or cold as a dip.

1 kg   (2 lb) pumpkin
1   teaspoon salt
3   garlic cloves, crushed
2   tablespoons lemon juice
1   tablespoon olive oil
1/4   teaspoon cayenne
1   tablespoon caraway seeds
1   teaspoon ground coriander

Peel and chop up the pumpkin. Cook in salted water for 20 minutes or until tender. Drain and put the pumpkin and all the other ingredients into a food processor and blend to a smooth purée. Serves 6.

Green Cabbage with Caraway

This is an Italian way of cooking cabbage.

1 kg	(2 lb) Savoy cabbage
2	tablespoons olive oil
1	large onion, chopped
4	garlic cloves, chopped
1/2	teaspoon salt
1	teaspoon pepper
1	tablespoon caraway seeds
2	tablespoons wine vinegar

Shred the cabbage finely. Heat the oil in a pan, add the onion and cook until it is starting to brown. Add garlic, cook for 1 minute, then add the cabbage, salt, pepper and caraway seeds. Keep stirring the cabbage until it has wilted. Add vinegar, stir, and cover the pan. Turn the heat very low and cook for 1 hour or until tender. Check very quickly several times to see that the liquid hasn't dried up and to turn the cabbage over. Serves 6.

CARDAMOM

CARDAMOM originally came from western India and was brought to Europe by Arab traders. It is a vital spice in Indian cuisine. It is best to buy the cardamom pods and split them open to obtain the seeds. Ground cardamom quickly loses its wonderful aromatic flavour and perfume. Use it to flavour curries, fruit cakes, biscuits, rice dishes, sweet and savoury.

Hazelnut Chicken

1	large chicken
FOR THE MARINADE	
125 ml	(4 fl oz) natural yoghurt
1	tablespoon ground cardamom
1	teaspoon ground cumin
1	teaspoon pepper
FOR THE STUFFING	
90 g	(3 oz) cups soft breadcrumbs
60 g	(2 oz) hazelnuts, chopped
1/2	teaspoon ground cardamom
1/2	teaspoon ground cumin
1	teaspoon pepper
1	tablespoon oil
1	onion, chopped
2	garlic cloves, chopped
1	egg

Wash and dry the chicken. Mix the marinade ingredients.

Combine the breadcrumbs, nuts and spices in a bowl. Heat the oil in a pan and add the onion. Cook until the onion is tender, then add the garlic and cook for a further minute. Strain and put the onion and garlic into the bowl. Add the egg and mix the stuffing. Pack it into the chicken and sew up cavity.

Place the chicken in a gratin dish. Using your fingers, open up the area between the skin and the flesh. Coat the flesh with three-quarters of the marinade. Coat the outside with the leftover marinade and leave to stand for 1 hour, covered. Place in a preheated oven (190°C; 375°F; gas 5) for an hour or until cooked. Baste every 15 minutes with the marinade. Serves 4.

A wonderful aromatic dish that is full of flavour and not too hot. Hazelnut chicken is a firm favourite with my family.

Fish with Cardamom

Any fish with firm white flesh will be suitable for this recipe. Serve with warm rice and salad.

4	fish steaks, about 2cm (3/4 in.) thick
1/2	teaspoon turmeric
4	onions,
10	garlic cloves, chopped
250 ml	(8 fl oz) natural yoghurt
1	teaspoon pepper
2	chillies, chopped
2	tablespoons oil
12	cardamom pods
4	cinnamon sticks

Wash and dry the fish. Sprinkle with turmeric and rub into the flesh.

Slice 3 of the onions finely. Put the fourth one, peeled and roughly chopped, into the food processor. Add the garlic, yoghurt, pepper and chillies. Blend to a smooth paste and reserve.

Put the oil in a pan and, when hot, add in the onion slices, cardamom and cinnamon. Cook until the onions are golden brown. Turn the heat down low and pour in the mixture from the food processor. Simmer for 10 minutes, stirring occasionally. Now add the fish steaks, scooping some of the sauce on top. They should be ready in 10 minutes, but test with the point of a knife–they are ready as soon as the flesh is no longer translucent. Serves 4.

CINNAMON

CINNAMON is native to Sri Lanka but is now grown in many other countries. It is sometimes confused with *cassia* which is similar and has been known in China and Egypt for thousands of years. They are both the bark of a tree which curls up into quills.

One of the most popular spices, ground cinnamon can be used to flavour puddings, chutneys, cakes, buns and curries. Use the bark for rice dishes, spiced wines, casseroles and for pickling fruits.

Pumpkin soup with a cinnamon flavour, thickened with long-grain rice. Perfect for a cold winter day. Serve with fresh crusty bread.

Pumpkin Soup

1 kg	(2 lb) pumpkin flesh, chopped
1	tablespoon oil
1	onion, chopped
1	teaspoon salt
1	teaspoon pepper
2	tablespoons ground cinnamon
1	tablespoon rosemary
315 ml	(1/2 pint) milk
185 g	(6 oz) cooked brown rice,
	Sprigs of parsley

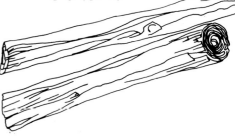

Heat the oil in a pan and add the pumpkin and onion. Stir until the onion is translucent, then cover with water. Add the salt, pepper, cinnamon and rosemary. Cook until the pumpkin is soft. Put the soup into a food processor and blend. Return to the heat and add the milk and rice. Cook until almost boiling. Garnish with parsley sprigs. Serves 4.

Apple Cake

155 g	(5 oz) butter
220 g	(7 oz) caster sugar
3	eggs
185 g	(6 oz) self-raising flour
500 g	(1 lb) apples
FOR THE GARNISH	
2	teaspoons ground cinnamon
1	teaspoon caster sugar
1	teaspoon ground almonds

Cut the butter into small pieces and beat in a bowl with the sugar, using an electric mixer, until white and fluffy. Now add the eggs, one at a time. Gradually add the flour, folding it in with a wooden spoon.

Peel and slice the apples. Put half the cake batter into a greased cake tin, 25cm (10 in.). Arrange half the apple slices over it and cover with the rest of the batter. Arrange the rest of the apple on top in a swirling pattern of apple slices. Mix together the cinnamon, sugar and almond. Sprinkle over the top of the cake.

Put in a preheated oven (180°C; 350°F; gas 4) for 40 minutes or until cooked. Test with a cocktail stick–if it comes out clean, the cake is ready. Remove from the oven, leave to stand for 15 minutes, then turn out onto a wire rack.

Cinnamon Hearts

If you don't have a heart-shaped biscuit cutter, trace the above pattern. Bake them for St. Valentine's Day or for your lover's birthday dinner.

8	egg whites
440 g	(14 oz) caster sugar
6	teaspoons ground cinnamon
220 g	(7 oz) ground almonds
2	teaspoons grated lemon zest
345 g	(11 oz) icing sugar

Beat the egg whites with an electric mixer until they are light and frothy. Gradually add the sugar and cinnamon. Keep beating until the mixture is very stiff.

Reserve half the mixture and to the other half add the almonds and lemon zest. Then work in the icing sugar, mixing well. Roll out the mixture to 3mm (1/8 in.) thickness. Cut into heart shapes and brush the tops with the reserved mixture. Put onto well greased baking trays and place in a preheated oven (180°C; 350°F; gas 4) for 20 minutes or until golden brown. Remove from the oven and cool on wire racks.

CLOVES

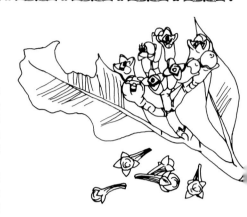

CLOVES originally came from South-East Asia and there is evidence to suggest they were being used by the Chinese several thousand years ago. The clove tree is now also grown in other tropical countries such as Zanzibar and the West Indies.

Cloves are a powerful antiseptic and should be used cautiously so as not to overpower other flavours. Always buy whole cloves and grind them yourself. They are indispensable in cooking spiced cakes and puddings, stewed fruits, curries and all kinds of stewed meat dishes.

Clove Meatballs

Serve these spicy balls as an appetiser.

1	small onion, chopped
3	garlic cloves, chopped
60 ml	(2 fl oz) lemon juice
1	tablespoon chopped ginger
1	teaspoon pepper
10	whole cloves
1	teaspoon cardamom seeds
2	chillies
4	tablespoons chickpea flour
1.25 kg	(2 1/2 lb) minced lamb
2	eggs
30 g	(1 oz) coriander leaves, chopped

Into the food processor put the onion, garlic, lemon juice, ginger, pepper, cloves, cardamom and chillies. Blend to a smooth paste. Reserve.

Put the chickpea flour into a pan and heat, stirring, until it darkens. Remove from the heat.

Put the meat and coriander leaves into a bowl, pour the paste from the food processor and add the chickpea flour. Mix well and leave to marinate for 4-10 hours in the refrigerator.

Add the eggs to the mixture and shape into small balls. Brush with oil and cook under a hot grill for 10 minutes or until done.

Split Pea Soup

315 g	(10 oz) split peas, washed
1 25 ltrs	(2 1/4 pints) chicken stock
1	onion, chopped
15	whole cloves (tied in muslin)
2	teaspoons pepper
1	teaspoon salt
2	tablespoons chopped parsley
1	tablespoon lemon juice

Soak the split peas overnight. The next morning, put peas, stock and onion in a saucepan then bring to the boil. Remove any scum from the surface.

Add the cloves, pepper and salt. Cover and simmer for 1 1/2 hours or until the peas are soft and disintegrating. Take out the muslin bag and squeeze the juices back into the soup. Blend the soup in the food processor if you want a smooth purée, but personally I prefer the textured soup. Sprinkle with parsley before serving.

Spiced grapes are really delicious to eat with coffee at the end of a meal.

16

Spiced Grapes

1 kg	(2 lb) large firm seedless grapes
315 g	(10 oz) caster sugar
6	whole cloves
10	black peppercorns
1	teaspoon coriander seeds
	Peel of half an orange
1	bottle of brandy

Wash and dry the grapes and cut them off the branches, leaving the stems on. Put them into a bowl, cover with the sugar, spices and lemon peel. Stir the grapes so that they are all coated.

Spoon into sterilised jars along with all the flavourings. Pour the brandy over to cover. Seal, label and store for 2 months. Shake the jars occasionally.

CORIANDER

CORIANDER is native to southern Europe and the Middle East but is now grown all over the world. Coriander has been used in cooking and as a medicine for thousands of years in Europe, India and China.

The dried seeds can be added whole to flavour curries and rice dishes, pickles and sausages. Freshly ground, they give an interesting flavour to cakes and fruit compotes, breads and pastries. Coriander is a basic and indispensable ingredient in spiced dishes from India, Malaya, Thailand and Indonesia.

Lentil Soup

375 g	(12 oz) lentils
2	onions, chopped
3	bacon rashers, chopped
185 g	(6 oz) carrots chopped
1	tablespoon oil
2 litres	(3 1/2 pints) stock
1	teaspoon salt
2	teaspoons pepper
1	tablespoon ground coriander
1	teaspoon ground cumin
3	tablespoons chopped mint leaves

Wash the lentils thoroughly and soak in water for several hours. Fry the onion and bacon in the oil until the onion is translucent. Add the drained lentils and carrots for a minute, stirring, then pour over the stock. Season with salt and pepper, coriander and cumin. Bring to the boil and simmer gently until the lentils are cooked. Garnish with mint leaves before serving. Serves 6-8.

Spiced Ham

An old-fashioned way of preparing and cooking ham.

3 kg	(6 lb) hand of pork
125 g	(4 oz) salt
2	teaspoons saltpetre
1	tablespoon black peppercorns
3	tablespoons coriander seeds
1	tablespoon allspice berries
125 g	(4 oz) dark brown sugar
1	onion, chopped
1	carrot, chopped
1	bouquet garni
125 ml	(4 fl oz) white wine
	Juice and zest of 1 orange
10	whole cloves

Grind salt, saltpetre, peppercorns, coriander and allspice together, then mix in the sugar.

Prick the pork all over with a sterilised carving fork. Rub the spice and salt into the pork. Put it into a sterilised dish the same size as the leg. Cover with a sterilised lid and leave in the refrigerator for 8 days. Bring it out every day and rub it with the spice and salt. The salt gradually draws moisture from the pork, so soon you will have juice to rub over the pork.

After 8 days, rinse and dry the pork thoroughly. In order to get rid of some of the salt, the pork into a saucepan of cold water and bring to the boil. Pour the water out and repeat the process.

In a baking dish just a little bigger than the pork, lay down the onion, carrot, bouquet garni and orange zest. Place the pork on top and stud with the cloves. Pour the wine and orange juice over it. Cover with a lid or two layers of foil and put it into a preheated oven (160°C; 325°F; gas 3) for 3 hours. Remove from the heat and keep covered while the ham cools down. Serves 10.

CUMIN

CUMIN originally came from the East but is now grown in warm countries all over the world. An ancient spice, the seeds have been used ·as a medicine as well as a flavouring for spiced dishes. The Mexicans used it to make chilli con carne and it is one of the most popular spices in Middle Eastern and North African cuisine. It is also essential for Indian dishes. Cumin adds flavour to breads, pickles and chutneys, rice, vegetable and meat dishes.

Opposite: This recipe makes the most delicious spiced ham I have ever tasted. Eat it hot or cold.

Cumin and tomato harmonise wonderfully together. Add a sprinkling of cayenne if you like.

Cumin & Tomato Salad

A refreshing salad to serve with curries and Middle Eastern food.

375 ml (12 fl oz) natural yoghurt
2   tablespoons lemon juice
1   tablespoon cumin seeds
4   tomatoes, chopped
2   garlic cloves, chopped
2   tablespoons coriander leaves
1   teaspoon paprika

Mix the yoghurt and lemon juice together in a bowl. Heat cumin seeds in a dry pan until they begin to smoke. Stir them into the yoghurt along with the tomatoes, garlic and coriander leaves. Mix well and garnish with paprika.

Lamb Kebabs

Serve these spicy kebabs with pitta bread and salads. They taste best grilled over a barbecue fire.

A shoulder of lamb
FOR THE MARINADE
2   tablespoons cumin seeds
1   tablespoon black peppercorns
1   teaspoon turmeric
1   tablespoon grated ginger
1   onion, finely chopped
3   garlic cloves, chopped
1   teaspoon salt
2   tablespoons chopped coriander leaves

Cut the lamb into bite-sized pieces and remove

the fat. Heat the cumin in a dry pan until it starts to smoke; grind the seeds in a food mill or coffee grinder along with the peppercorns. Put them into a bowl with the turmeric, ginger, onion, garlic, salt and coriander. Mix well together and marinate the meat for several hours. Just before cooking, thread the lamb onto skewers and grill, basting with the marinade as you turn.

GINGER

GINGER grows in moist tropical conditions in many countries, though it originally came from South-East Asia. It is used fresh, preserved in syrup or ground after drying. It is one of the most popular condiments for cakes such as gingerbread and ginger snaps, for drinks like ginger beer and ginger wine, and for all manner of desserts. It is an essential ingredient in many Chinese, Indian, Japanese and Korean dishes.

Ginger Cake

This is a very moist, rich ginger cake that will last a fortnight. For an attractive topping, place a doily on the cooled cake and gently rub icing sugar through a sieve, sprinkling it over the surface of the cake. When you remove the doily, you will reveal a lacy pattern.

155 g	(5 oz) butter
125 g	(4 oz) dark brown sugar
2	eggs
250 g	(8 oz) flour
2	teaspoons ground ginger
1	teaspoon salt
315 g	(10 oz) golden syrup
125 g	(4 oz) raisins
1/2	teaspoon bicarbonate of soda
75 ml	(2 1/2 fl oz) milk, warmed

Beat the butter until it is light and fluffy. Add the sugar and beat until light. Beat in the eggs, one at a time. Fold in the flour, ginger and salt. Then stir in the golden syrup and raisins. Add the bicarbonate of soda to the milk and gently stir it into the cake mixture.

Grease a 20cm (8 in.) cake tin. Pour the mixture in and place in a preheated oven (180°C; 350°F; gas 4). Bake for 1 1/2 hours. If the top is getting too brown, turn the oven down for the last 30 minutes. Remove from the oven. After 10 minutes, turn the cake out onto a rack.

Mango & Date Chutney

125 g	(4 oz) mango, chopped
155 g	(5 oz) dates, pitted and chopped
2	tablespoons chopped ginger
1	tablespoon ground ginger
60 g	(2 oz) sultanas
1	tablespoon ground allspice
3	chillies, chopped
155 ml	(1/4 pint) vinegar
220 g	(7 oz) granulated sugar

Put the mango, dates, ginger, sultanas, allspice, chillies and vinegar into a saucepan and bring to the boil. Add the sugar and stir until it has dissolved. Simmer for about 30 minutes or until the chutney is not liquid any more, but a thick consistency. You should be able to draw a wooden spoon along the bottom of the saucepan without seeing free liquid. Spoon into warm sterilised jars, seal and store in a cool, dark place for a month before opening.

Blueberry & Ginger Crumble

This is an unusual combination of ginger and blueberries. Really delicious to make in summer when blueberries come into the shops. Serve cold with cream or yoghurt if you wish, but it is excellent unadorned.

500 g	(1 lb) blueberries
2	tablespoons caster sugar
155 g	(5 oz) butter, softened
250 g	(8 oz) flour
60 g	(2 oz) dark brown sugar
90 g	(3 oz) caster sugar
1/2	teaspoon bicarbonate of soda
2	teaspoons ground ginger

Put the blueberries into a pie dish and sprinkle with the caster sugar. To prepare the crumble, mix the butter and flour together with your fingers until the mixture resembles breadcrumbs. Add the sugars, bicarbonate of soda and ginger. Cover the blueberries lightly with this mixture, making sure it is level, but don't press it down. Bake in a preheated oven (180°C; 350°F; gas 4) for 30 minutes. Serves 6.

JUNIPER

JUNIPER is native to many parts of Europe, either as a shrub or a tree. The berries are very aromatic, so they should be used sparingly. Crush 5-9 seeds to put in wine or spiced marinades for meats and poultry, and to flavour sauerkraut and pâtés.

Spiced Pork

	A leg of pork, boned
20	juniper berries, crushed
1	tablespoon salt
1	tablespoon black peppercorns
3	garlic cloves, chopped
2	pig's trotters
6	bay leaves
6	fennel stalks
1	orange, sliced with skin left on
1	carrot
250 ml	(8 fl oz) white wine
125 ml	(4 fl oz) sherry

Mix the juniper berries, salt, pepper and garlic together. Prick the pork with a skewer and rub the spices all over. Leave to marinate for 24 hours in the refrigerator. Into a large pot put the trotters, bay leaves, fennel, orange, carrot and white wine. Lay the pork on top and cover with cold water. Put the lid on and place in a preheated oven (150°C; 300°F; gas 2) for 3 hours. Test with a skewer to see if it is cooked –the skewer should penetrate easily.

Remove the pork and place on a serving dish. To make the jelly, put the stock back into the oven to cook for a few more hours to be sure to obtain a good jelly. Pour the stock through a sieve into a bowl. Refrigerate. The next day, the fat will have set on top. Remove it and reduce the stock over a high heat to about 500 ml (16 fl oz). Remove from the heat

A refreshing dessert after a rich, heavy meal. Spicy orange dessert is easy to make and not too time-consuming.

and add the sherry. Pour into a greased jelly mould or bowl and leave to set. Turn it out just before serving the pork. Serves 12.

MACE

MACE is the dried outer coat of the nutmeg pod. The nutmeg tree is native to Indonesia and the Philippines. The flavour is similar to nutmeg but a little more refined. Use it to flavour soups and stews, sausages, pies, pickles, sauces and cakes. Buy it whole and grind it just before using.

Spicy Orange Dessert

4	blades of mace
1	cinnamon stick
1	piece of vanilla pod
5	whole cloves
375 ml	(12 fl oz) white wine
90 g	(3 oz) caster sugar
6	oranges
60 g	(2 oz) flaked almonds

Put the spices, wine and sugar into a saucepan and bring to the boil. Simmer for 15 minutes. Peel and slice the oranges and arrange them in a bowl. When the liquid has cooled pour it over the oranges. Garnish with flaked almonds before serving. Serves 6.

Overleaf: Peanut sauce for satay (p. 45) to serve with chicken satay (p. 44). Thai curry paste in the foreground (p. 31).

23

Crunchy chicken drumsticks. They are extra special cooked on the barbecue with whole sweetcorn and jacket potatoes.

Bean & Lamb Casserole

A hearty, rustic casserole. The lamb is so tender and soft that a knife will be superfluous.

	A shoulder of lamb
500 g	*(1 lb) haricot beans*
30 g	*(1 oz) parsley, chopped*
6	*garlic cloves, crushed*
2	*tablespoons tomato purée*
2	*teaspoons ground mace*
1	*teaspoon ground cinnamon*
1/2	*teaspoon ground cloves*
2	*teaspoons pepper*

Soak beans overnight. Cut the flesh from the lamb in thin strips, 5cm (2 in.) wide and 12cm (5 in.) long. Mix together the parsley, garlic, tomato purée and spices. Rub the meat with the spice mixture, and marinate for 4 hours or overnight. Roll up the lamb strips and place them in a casserole.

Strain the beans, place in a pan of cold water and bring to the boil. Boil rapidly for 10 minutes, then strain and put them on top of the meat. Cover with water, put the lid on and cook in a preheated oven (120°C; 250°F; gas 1/2) for 5 hours. Serves 4.

MUSTARD

MUSTARD has been known as a spice for thousands of years. It has also been used as a digestive and a medicine. There are three types of seeds. *Nigra*, or black, mustard originated in the Middle East which is the most pungent. *Juncea*, or brown, mustard is from China, India and Poland. The seeds are not quite as strong as the *Nigra*. *Alba*, or white, mustard is native to the Mediterranean and is a milder flavour.

Mustard, as we know it, is basically a paste made from seeds combined with herbs, spices, honey, vinegar or wine. Mustard is used to flavour sauces; vegetables and salads; fish, poultry and meat dishes; pickles and chutneys.

Mustard Butter

A useful butter to have on hand for marinating fish and meats before grilling or barbecuing.

4	teaspoons green peppercorns
4	teaspoons Dijon mustard
155 g	(5 oz) butter, melted
1	tablespoon finely chopped parsley
1	tablespoon finely chopped chives

Mix all the ingredients thoroughly in a bowl. Pour any of the mustard butter not needed into ice-cube trays and freeze.

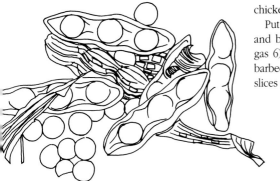

Chicken with Mustard

A delicious way to eat chicken with the crisp crunchy texture of breadcrumbs.

8	chicken drumsticks
2	tablespoons wholegrain mustard
185 g	(6 oz) dry breadcrumbs
1	teaspoon salt
1	teaspoon pepper
90 g	(3 oz) butter
90 g	(3 oz) flour
2	eggs, beaten
FOR THE LIME & MUSTARD BUTTER	
155 g	(5 oz) butter
1	tablespoon Dijon mustard
	A squeeze of lime juice
1/4	teaspoon cayenne

Make the lime and mustard butter a few hours ahead of cooking time. Cream the butter until soft, then gradually beat in the mustard, lime juice and cayenne. Roll it into a log shape and wrap in greaseproof paper. Refrigerate until needed.

Remove the skin from the chicken. Mix the wholegrain mustard, breadcrumbs, salt and pepper. Melt the butter in a saucepan and add the breadcrumb mixture. Stir until all the breadcrumbs are coated with butter. Remove from the heat and leave to cool.

Put the flour into a bowl. Beat the eggs in another bowl. Take each drumstick and first coat with flour, then dip into the beaten egg, and lastly press the breadcrumbs over the chicken.

Put the drumsticks on a greased baking tray and bake in a preheated oven (200°C; 400°F; gas 6) for 45 minutes. Alternatively, cook on a barbecue. Cut the lime and mustard butter into slices and serve with the chicken. Serves 4.

NUTMEG

Plum Soup

A spicy fruit soup starter of a summer dinner.

1 kg	(2 lb) plums, washed and stemmed
2	tablespoons fine tapioca
1.5 ltrs	(2 3/4 pints) chicken stock
500 ml	(16 fl oz) sweet white wine
90 g	(3 oz) caster sugar
2	chillies
3	whole cloves
1	lemon, finely sliced
1	teaspoon salt
1	teaspoon grated nutmeg
4	lemon slices

THE NUTMEG tree is native to Indonesia and the Philippines. For the best flavour, always buy the whole seed and grate it freshly when needed. It can be used in sweet and savoury

dishes such as cakes and puddings, egg and cheese dishes, sausages and curries, spinach and pumpkin.

Opposite: This delicately flavoured soup tastes as beautiful as it looks. I take the skins off the plums to give the soup a pale colour.

Dissolve the tapioca by bringing 500 ml (16 fl oz) of chicken stock to the boil, reducing to a simmer and then gradually adding the tapioca. Stirring constantly, continue to simmer until it is translucent. Put plums into a large saucepan with the rest of the stock, wine, sugar, chillies, cloves and lemon. Bring to the boil and simmer until the plums are tender. Remove the plums, lemon slices and chillies. Skin the plums, cut them in half and take out the stones. Return the plums to the soup. Add the salt and nutmeg. Add the tapioca and stock mixture. Serve chilled with half a slice of lemon in each bowl. Serves 8.

Baked Spinach

This delightful vegetable dish makes a lovely lunch. Serve with a tomato salad and crusty bread.

750 g	(1 1/2 lb) spinach
90 g	(3 oz) long-grain rice
5	eggs
315 ml	(1/4 pint) milk
1	teaspoon salt
1	teaspoon pepper
1	teaspoon grated nutmeg
1	teaspoon lemon juice

Wash the spinach leaves well and chop finely. Cook them in boiling water until wilted. Drain. Put the rice into a saucepan with 250 ml (8 fl oz) of water. Bring to the boil, cover and turn the heat to low. The rice should be cooked in 20 minutes. Stir gently and fluff up.

Beat the eggs lightly and gradually stir in the milk, salt, pepper, nutmeg and lemon juice. Add the spinach and rice, then pour the mixture into a gratin dish. Put into a preheated oven (190°C; 375°F; gas 5) for 30 minutes or until it is set. Serves 4.

Potatoes with Nutmeg

These potatoes taste excellent with roast chicken. Nutmeg and potato have a great affinity.

500 g   (1 lb) potatoes
375 ml (12 fl oz) milk
1   teaspoon grated nutmeg
1   teaspoon salt
1   teaspoon pepper
*   Zest of half a lemon*

Slice the potatoes thickly and arrange in a gratin dish. Pour the milk over and sprinkle with the spices and lemon zest. Put into a preheated oven (180°C; 350°F; gas 4) for 1 1/4 hours. Serves 6.

PEPPER, CHILLI, CAYENNE & PAPRIKA

THERE are two different types of spice that are called pepper–peppercorns on the one hand and chilli, cayenne and paprika on the other. Peppercorns grow on a vine that is native to the monsoon areas of Asia. They are a basic ingredient in most of the world's cuisine's. Always buy peppercorns whole and grind them as required. Pepper adds interest to almost any dish.

Chilli, cayenne and paprika come from the sweet pepper or capsicum family. It is believed they originally came from South America. Chillies are the most pungent of the family but even their varieties differ in strength from mild

Pepper & Garlic Chicken

Serve this peppery chicken with rice and a cooling yoghurt salad.

1   chicken
FOR THE MARINADE
2   tablespoons pepper
10   garlic cloves, crushed
1   teaspoon salt
30 g   (1 oz) mint leaves, chopped
125 ml   (4 fl oz) orange juice

Cut the chicken into ten pieces, and remove the fat and the skin if you wish. Put the rest of the ingredients into a food processor and blend to a smooth paste. Rub it all over the chicken and leave to marinate for at least 4 hours in the refrigerator.

Cook under the grill or on the barbecue, brushing with the marinade every time you turn the chicken. Serves 6.

to explosive. Green or red, they can be used fresh, dried, whole or ground.

Cayenne pepper is made from a ground red chilli pepper which originally came from Cayenne in French Guyana.

Ground paprika pepper comes from a special variety of pepper, much milder than the pungent chilli. It is a brilliant red colour and is the most popular spice in Spanish, Portuguese and Hungarian cooking.

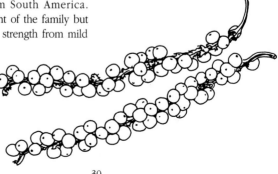

Pear Pie

Spend some time decorating the top of your pie to give it a really spectacular appearance.

1.5 kg	(3 lb) pears, peeled, cored and cut into 8 pieces each
4	tablespoons white rum
2	tablespoons lemon juice
440 g	(14 oz) caster sugar
1	tablespoon pepper
1	teaspoon ground cinnamon
410 g	(13 oz) frozen puff pastry, thawed
1	egg, beaten
125 ml	(4 fl oz) double cream

Put the pears into a bowl with the rum, lemon juice, sugar, pepper and cinnamon and leave them to soak.

Roll out two-thirds of the pastry to a thickness of 3mm (1/8 in.). Butter and flour a pie tin and line it with pastry. Drain the pears, reserving the juice, and arrange them in the pie. Put a pie funnel in the centre to let out the steam.

Roll out the rest of the pastry and cover the pie. Pinch the edges together and decorate the top with some leftover pastry. Cut a hole around the pie funnel. Brush the pastry with the beaten egg.

Put the pie into a preheated oven at 180°C (350°F; gas 4) and cook for 45-60 minutes until the pie is golden brown. Stir the cream into the pear juice and pour it through the hole in the pastry lid. Serves 8.

Moroccan Stew

1 kg	(2 lb) boned shoulder or leg of lamb
2	tablespoons oil
1	tablespoon pepper
1/2	teaspoon turmeric
1/2	teaspoon ground cinnamon
3	garlic cloves, crushed
2	onions, finely chopped
500 g	(1 lb) dried apricots
2	teaspoons cumin seeds
2	tablespoons clear honey
2	tablespoons orange juice
60 g	(2 oz) flaked almonds
1	tablespoon oil

Trim the meat of fat and cut into large pieces. Heat the oil in a saucepan and brown the onions and meat. Stir in the spices and garlic and mix well. Add enough water to cover the meat. Simmer, with the lid on, for 1 1/2 hours.

Meanwhile, soak the apricots and cumin in the honey and orange juice. When the meat is tender, add the fruit and cook for another 15 minutes. At the same time, fry the almonds in oil to sprinkle on top of the casserole when serving. Serves 6.

Thai Curry Paste

Keeping a jar of Thai curry paste in the refrigerator ensures a quick curry.

10	red chillies
3	onions, chopped
1	teaspoon Laos powder
1	tablespoon chopped ginger
1	tablespoon chopped lemon grass
	Zest of 2 limes
2	tablespoons oil

Put all the ingredients into a food processor and blend to a smooth paste. Store in a sealed jar in the refrigerator.

Thai beef curry is best cooked in a wok.

Thai Beef Curry

1 kg	(2 lb) rump steak
1	tablespoon oil
3	tablespoons Thai curry paste (p. 31)
6	chillies
750 ml	(24 fl oz) water
125 ml	(4 fl oz) coconut cream
2	tablespoons fish sauce
1	tablespoon caster sugar
30 g	(1 oz) basil leaves

Slice the beef very thinly. Heat the oil in a wok or pan and fry the curry paste for 1 minute. Add the water and coconut cream and bring to the boil. Add the meat slices and chillies and cook for 10 minutes. Add the fish sauce, sugar and basil, stir and serve immediately with steamed rice and salad. Serves 6.

Chilli Prawns with Whole Spices

A spicy way to cook prawns. Serve with plenty of steamed rice and a cool yoghurt or fresh chutney. You get a much tastier prawn by keeping the shell, head and tail on.

1.5 kg	(3 lb) green prawns
2	tablespoons oil
1	cinnamon stick
6	cardamom pods
2	whole cloves
1/2	teaspoon turmeric
2	bay leaves
4	chillies

FOR THE MARINADE
6	garlic cloves
2	tablespoons chopped ginger
6	chillies
2	tablespoons lemon juice

De-vein the prawns by cutting the shell along the back and removing the intestine. Wash and dry the prawns.

Put the marinade ingredients into a food processor. Blend to a sooth paste. Pour paste over the prawns, cover and marinate for 1 to 4 hours in the refrigerator.

Heat the oil in a wok or pan. Add the spices, bay leaves and chillies and cook until bay leaves change colour. Drain the marinade from the prawns and put into the wok. Stir-fry until paste thickens. Add the prawns and stir fry for 5 minutes or until just cooked. Serves 6.

The most delicious way I know of cooking prawns. The flesh steams inside the shell and still retains the flavour of the marinade. Have plenty of paper napkins handy because it is best to eat with your fingers.

Baked Fish

Any sweet white fish will go with this interesting marinade from the Middle East. Serve rice or couscous with cumin & tomato salad (p. 20).

8	white fish fillets
FOR THE MARINADE	
2	tablespoons paprika
3	chillies, chopped
3	teaspoons ground allspice
10	garlic cloves, chopped
75 ml	(2 1/2 fl oz) lemon juice
30 g	(1 oz) coriander leaves, chopped
3	tablespoons mint leaves, chopped
125 ml	(4 fl oz) olive oil
1	teaspoon salt
2	teaspoons pepper
	Lemon wedges

Mix all the marinade ingredients together and pour over the fish fillets. Cover and marinade in the refrigerator for 5 hours if possible. Place under a preheated grill. Turn only once. When the fish is no longer translucent it is ready. It is better to undercook fish slightly than dry it out by overcooking. Garnish with lemon wedges. Serves 4.

Paprika Cabbage

A German way of cooking cabbage. It looks very attractive served on white plates.

750 g	(1 1/2 lb) cabbage
FOR THE MARINADE	
125 ml	(4 fl oz) white vinegar
1	tablespoon caraway seeds
1	tablespoon salt
1	tablespoon pepper
2	tablespoons paprika
2	onions, sliced
125 g	(4 oz) butter
125 ml	(4 fl oz) white wine

Salsa Fresca

A hot fresh sauce from Mexico. Use as a dip for corn chips and crudités or as a sauce for grilled meats or meatballs.

3	large tomatoes, chopped
3	tablespoons chopped coriander leaves
1	onion, chopped
6	chillies, chopped
4	tablespoons lemon juice
1	teaspoon salt

Put all the ingredients into a food processor and blend to a smooth sauce.

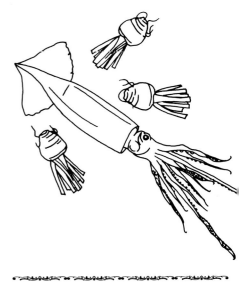

Shred the cabbage. Combine all the ingredients for the marinade and mix through the cabbage. Cover and refrigerate for 12 hours. Drain off the vinegar.

Melt butter in a large saucepan, add the onion slices and cook until they are translucent. Add the cabbage and paprika and stir thoroughly. Add the wine and cook, covered, for 1 hour. Serves 6.

Devilled Almonds

155 g (5 oz) blanched almonds
1 teaspoon oil
1 teaspoon salt
1/4 teaspoon cayenne

Coat the almonds with the oil. Spread them out on an oiled baking tray and put into a pre-heated oven (180°C; 350°F; gas 4). Turn the almonds occasionally and cook until they are golden brown. Remove from heat and sprinkle with the salt and cayenne. Serve hot or cold, but they are best the day they are made.

Squid with Vegetables

An unusual combination of squid, turnips, tomatoes and spinach from North Africa.

750 g (1 1/2 lb) baby squid
1 tablespoon oil
1 onion, chopped
500 g (1 lb) small turnips, quartered
125 g (4 oz) tomatoes, chopped
1 teaspoon grated nutmeg
1 teaspoon pepper
1/4 teaspoon cayenne
250 ml (8 fl oz) water
500 g (1 lb) spinach
30 g (1 oz) parsley, chopped

Ask the fishmonger to clean the squid for you. Cut them into bite-sized pieces. Heat the oil in the pan and add the onion. Cook until it is soft, then add the turnips, tomatoes, nutmeg, pepper, cayenne and water. Simmer for 15 minutes. Stir in the spinach and when it has wilted, add the squid. The squid will be ready as soon as it becomes opaque. Serve immediately. Serves 6.

SAFFRON

SAFFRON is the dried or ground *stigma* from the *saffron crocus*. It is the rarest and most expensive of spices as it needs approximately a quarter of a million flowers to produce 500 g (1 lb) of saffron. It is important to many Spanish, Italian and French dishes. In India it is only used for festive occasions. Saffron enhances cakes and bread, fish, chicken and rice dishes.

Saffron Chicken

1 chicken
1/3 teaspoon ground saffron
     or 1/2 teaspoon saffron threads
2 tablespoons butter
1 tablespoon oil
2 onions, chopped
4 garlic cloves, crushed
250 ml (8 fl oz) natural yoghurt
125 g (4 oz) tomatoes, chopped
30 g (1 oz) coriander leaves, chopped
1 teaspoon salt
1 teaspoon pepper

Cut chicken into 10 pieces and remove the fat and skin. Dissolve saffron in 75 ml (2 1/2 fl oz) hot water. Heat the butter and oil and fry the onions until they are translucent. Remove onions and then brown the chicken pieces, adding more oil if necessary. Remove the chicken, and put in the garlic, yoghurt, tomatoes, half the coriander, salt and pepper. Stir for 5 minutes, then replace the chicken pieces. Add the saffron and stir well so the chicken is coated with the mixture. Cover and simmer for 50-60 minutes. Serve with the rest of the coriander sprinkled over the dish. Serves 6.

Risotto alla Milanese

A classic risotto which can be served alone as a starter or to accompany a main dish (the best known being Osso Bucco). Use a strong home-made chicken stock as that is the main flavouring along with the saffron. If available, use the plump Italian arborio rice which is ideally suited to risotto.

1 litre	(1 3/4 pints) chicken stock
30 g	(1 oz) butter
1	tablespoon oil
2	tablespoons chopped Parma ham
2	tablespoons chopped onion
315 g	(10 oz) arborio rice
1/3	teaspoon ground saffron
	or 1/2 teaspoon saffron threads
1	teaspoon pepper
30 g	(1 oz) parmesan cheese, grated

Bring the chicken stock to the boil and let it simmer very slowly. Dissolve the saffron in 2 tablespoons of hot stock. Put the butter and oil into a heavy-bottomed saucepan. Add the onions and Parma ham and fry until the onions are translucent. Add the rice and stir until all the grains are glistening. Pour over a ladleful of stock and stir. The risotto will take about 25 minutes to cook. As the rice absorbs the liquid, add more stock, stirring every few minutes.

After 15 minutes add the saffron. Test the rice to see if it is ready after 20 minutes. It should not be too soft, just a little firm or *al dente*. Remove from heat and mix in the pepper and cheese. Serve with extra cheese, if liked, for guests to add themselves. Serves 6.

SALT

COMMON SALT, or sodium chloride, is one of the minerals essential to life. It occurs naturally in sea water and is found in mineral deposits on land where ancient lakes and seas have dried up. It is a preservative as well as a condiment. It brings out the flavours of the food it is added to.

In cooking, it is better to use too little rather than too much. As it occurs naturally in much of the food we eat, it is not necessary to add large quantities, if any at all. Sea salt is superior and is recommended both for cooking and as a condiment.

*Simple but rich, **risotto alla Milanese** is a favourite Italian dish. Be sparing with the saffron as its slightly fishy flavour can become overwhelming.*

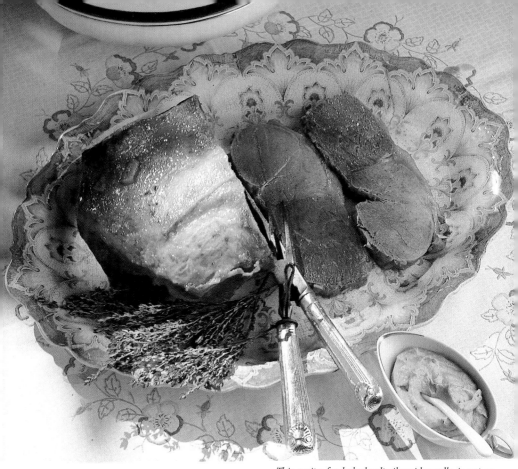

This recipe for baked salt silverside really is not as complicated as it looks and you will be rewarded with a wonderful flavour.

Trout Grilled with Salt

A Japanese way to cook whole any small salt-water or freshwater fish.

125 g	(4 oz) salt
6	small trout
1	tablespoon oil

FOR THE SAUCE

1	tablespoon grated horseradish
1	tablespoon tomato purée
1	tablespoon lime juice
1	tablespoon chopped dill
250 ml	(8 fl oz) mayonnaise

Ask your fishmonger to gut the fish. Wash them well under a running tap and dry with kitchen paper. Rub salt all over the outside and inside of the trout. Leave to marinate for 30 minutes.

In the meantime, make the sauce by combining all the ingredients in a bowl. Oil the grill pan and put the fish under a very hot grill. Turn after 5 minutes. The fish should be ready after another 5. Test with the point of a knife.
Serves 6.

Baked Salt Silverside

Salt the beef yourself for a change and taste the difference! Marinate it in the refrigerator for 5-7 days. A good butcher will usually give you some saltpetre.

2.5 kg	(5 lb) silverside of beef
1	onion
2	carrots
1	orange, halved
3	bay leaves
	A small bunch of parsley
1	tablespoon pepper
1	tablespoon ground ginger
1	tablespoon ground cinnamon
1	tablespoon cumin seeds
1	tablespoon mustard seeds

FOR THE BRINE

625 g	(1 1/4 lb) salt
185 g	(6 oz) dark brown sugar
2	teaspoons saltpetre
1.5 ltrs	(2 3/4 pints) water

Put all the brine ingredients into the saucepan and bring to the boil. Boil for about 20 minutes. Strain into the bowl in which you will marinate the beef. When the brine is cold, wash the beef and put it into the brine. Cover and refrigerate for 5 to 7 days.

Remove the beef from the brine and soak it in fresh water for a few hours. Put the beef into deep casserole dish, not much bigger than the beef. Add the onion, carrots, orange, bay leaves, parsley and spices. Add water to cover the beef. Bring water to the boil on top of the stove. Put the lid on and place in a preheated oven (180°C; 350°F; gas 4) for 3 hours or until the beef is tender. Eat hot or, if you want to eat it cold, place it in a bowl with a weight on top to compress the meat and make it easier to carve. Serves 10-12.

SESAME

THE SESAME SEED comes from an annual plant, a native of India. It is valued for its oily seeds and a paste called *tahina*. The Chinese, Indians and Mexicans value the oil highly for cooking. The nutty seeds can be toasted or dry - fried to use as a garnish for seafood, breads, sweets and cakes. Tahina paste is thick and smooth and made into *meze* which is a Middle Eastern word for starter or dip. Combine it with yoghurt, puréed white beans or with puréed aubergine to make baba ghanoush.

Baba Ghanoush

A most delicious dip from the Middle East made with aubergine and tahina paste made from crushed sesame seeds. If you have never tasted homemade baba ghanoush you have missed a wonderful treat.

3	large aubergines
4	garlic cloves, crushed
1	teaspoon salt
125 ml	(4 fl oz) tahina paste
125 ml	(4 fl oz) lemon juice
1	teaspoon cumin seeds

FOR THE GARNISH

	Parsley leaves
10	olives

Cut the aubergines in half and put them on an oiled baking tray. Bake in a preheated oven (190°C; 375°F; gas 5) for 45 minutes. Allow to cool. Scrape the flesh away from the skin and put into a food processor. Add the garlic, salt, tahina paste, lemon and cumin.

Blend to a smooth paste. It is traditional to serve the dip on a flat plate decorated with parsley leaves and olives.

Chinese Sesame Prawns

Prawns retain more flavour if cooked in their shell. It is worth the trouble of cleaning them.

1 kg	(2 lb) green prawns
4	garlic cloves, crushed
2	tablespoons chopped spring onions
75 ml	(2 1/2 fl oz) soy sauce
75 ml	(2 1/2 fl oz) dry sherry
2	tablespoons clear honey
2	tablespoons oil
2	tablespoons sesame seeds

De-vein the prawns by cutting along the back, through the shell and into the prawn-just deep enough to take the vein out. Keep the heads and tails on and wash thoroughly. Dry on kitchen paper.

Combine the garlic, spring onions, soy, sherry, honey and mix well. Heat the oil in a wok. Add the soy mixture and stir for a few minutes, then add the prawns, stirring constantly. Stir-fry for about 7 minutes or until the prawns are opaque. At the same time, dry-roast the sesame seeds. Serve at once with the sesame seeds sprinkled over the prawns. Serves 4.

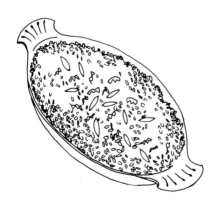

TURMERIC

TURMERIC is a rhizome that is dried and ground. It is native to India and South-East Asia. It is used in curries and rice dishes in India and the Middle East as much for its bright yellow colour as for its rather bitter flavour. It may also be used for fish kedgerees, devilled eggs, salad dressings and seafood stews.

Spiced Rice

250 g	(8 oz) long-grain rice
2 .	tablespoons oil
3	tablespoons chopped spring onions
750 ml	(24 fl oz) chicken stock
375 g	(12 oz) tomatoes, skinned and diced
250 g	(8 oz) peas, shelled
6	cardamom pods
1	tablespoon cumin seeds
1	tablespoon coriander seeds
1/4	teaspoon cayenne
6	whole cloves
1	tablespoon black peppercorns
1	teaspoon salt
2	bay leaves
FOR THE GARNISH	
60 g	(2 oz) flaked almonds
3	tablespoons chopped coriander leaves

Wash the rice and soak it in water for 30 minutes. Drain the rice and heat the oil in a wok or a large pan. Add the spring onions and stir-fry for a minute. Add the rice and coat all over with the oil. Now add the stock, tomatoes, peas, spices and bay leaves. Stir well and, when the stock comes to the boil, stir again, then cover and leave to cook on the lowest heat for an hour. Fluff up the rice and garnish with almonds and coriander leaves.

VANILLA

VANILLA bean is a pod from a climbing orchid, a native of tropical South America. The Aztecs used it to flavour chocolate. To obtain the true flavour use a vanilla pod or part of it, or make vanilla sugar. The pod can be used again and again until it has lost its pungency. Store it in the sugar jar. It is added to give flavour to ice-creams, custards, pastry and fruit dishes.

The dough for the walnut biscuits tastes and smells so delicious it is a wonder any biscuits ever get to be baked!

Walnut Biscuits

90 g	*(3 oz) walnut halves*
220 g	*(7 oz) vanilla sugar*
125 ml	*(4 fl oz) oil*
90 g	*(3 oz) butter*
1	*teaspoon lemon extract*
1/4	*teaspoon salt*
250 g	*(8 oz) self-raising flour*

Toast the walnuts and, when cool, grind in a food processor. Add the sugar, oil and butter to the walnuts and mix well. Then add the lemon extract, salt and flour, and blend until the mixture is smooth. Roll the dough into walnut-sized balls and put onto a well greased baking tray. Bake in a preheated oven (190°C; 375°F; gas 5) for 30 minutes or until the biscuits are cooked. Leave to cool on a wire rack.

Vanilla Sugar

Make vanilla sugar by simply putting a vanilla pod into a screw-top jar of granulated or caster sugar. Keep topping up with more sugar as it gets used. It will last for years and is the most economical way to obtain vanilla flavouring.

MIXED SPICES

MANY different cuisine's have their own combination of spices. The French use *Fines épices* which is a mixture of pepper, chilli, mace, nutmeg, cloves, cinnamon, bay leaves, sage, marjoram and rosemary, and *Quatre épices*, which is a combination of ground cloves, cinnamon, nutmeg and pepper, generally used for terrines, pâtés and hearty meat dishes. *Four Spices* in North Africa means pepper, rosebuds, cinnamon and paprika. *Chinese Five Spices* is a well-known flavouring and is a mixture of star anise, fennel, cloves, cinnamon and anise pepper. *Mixed Spices* is a ground mixture of allspice, cloves, nutmeg, cinnamon and ginger. *Pickling Spice* is generally a combination of mustard seed, dried chilli, peppercorns, allspice berries, cloves, mace and coriander seeds. Sometimes spices are roasted and then ground, like the Indian *masalas,* or cooked in oil to preserve them as spicy pastes, such as *Thai Curry Paste* (page 31).

Buy whole seeds and pods, roast and grind them yourself in a powerful electric grinder and store them in a screw-top jar. In the refrigerator they will keep for up to 6 months.

It is worthwhile buying the finest quality whole spices to grind yourself as needed. From the top clockwise, turmeric, stick of cinnamon, fresh chillies, coriander seeds, cardamom pods, cloves, fresh ginger root and cumin.

French Mixed Spices

A French recipe for a combination of spices and herbs, to be used to flavour hearty country soups, terrines and casseroles.

1	tablespoon dried thyme
˙1	tablespoon dried basil
1/2	tablespoon dried sage
5	dried bay leaves
1	tablespoon ground coriander
1	tablespoon ground mace
3	tablespoons pepper

Combine all the ingredients and mix well. Store in a screw-top jar.

Tandoori Marinade

There are many ways of making tandori marinade–this is my well-tested recipe. Cooking in a covered barbecue will give you the closest idea of how it tasted originally when cooked in the pear-shaped clay ovens.

250 ml	(8 fl oz) natural yoghurt
1	onion, finely chopped
6	garlic cloves , chopped
1	tablespoon chopped root ginger
2	chillies
	Juice of 1 lemon
2	tablespoons garam masala
1	teaspoon salt
1	tablespoon pepper
1	teaspoon turmeric or red food colouring

Put all the ingredients in a food processor and blend to a smooth paste. Marinate meat, poultry or seafood for at least 2 hours. Thread the meat onto skewers or, if cooking larger pieces, put them whole under a hot grill or on a barbecue. Baste continually while cooking and turning. Red food colouring gives a more authentic look, but I prefer the natural colour.

Thai Marinade

A spicy marinade for satay sticks. Serve with the peanut recipe that follows. Accompany with vegetable crudités and steamed rice.

1	teaspoon Thai curry paste (p. 31)
3	garlic cloves , chopped
1	tablespoon soy sauce
1	tablespoon chopped lemon grass
125 ml	(4 fl oz) coconut milk

Put all ingredients into a food processor and blend to a smooth paste. Marinate beef, pork, lamb or chicken for at least 2 hours. Thread onto skewers and grill. You can make a larger quantity and keep it refrigerated in a sealed jar.

Curry Powder

This curry powder should last for 6 months refrigerated. If you haven't tasted homemade curry powder made with freshly ground spices before, you will enjoy the difference.

4	tablespoons coriander seeds
2	tablespoons cumin seeds
2	tablespoons cardamom seeds
1	teaspoon fenugreek
1	tablespoon turmeric
1	tablespoon black peppercorns
1	tablespoon whole cloves
10	dried chillies

Grind all the spices finely and mix together well. Store in airtight containers.

Peanut Sauce for Satay

Serve this delicious sauce with satays or to accompany vegetable crudités. You can substitute peanut butter if you haven't time to roast and grind the peanuts yourself. There is a difference in flavour, though.

315 g   (10 oz) raw shelled peanuts
1   small onion, thinly sliced
1   tablespoon oil
3   garlic cloves, chopped
3   chillies
250 ml   (8 fl oz) water
1/4   teaspoon cayenne
1/2   teaspoon caster sugar
1/2   teaspoon salt
1   tablespoon soy sauce
1   tablespoon lemon juice

Place peanuts in a pan and roast in preheated oven at 190°C (375°F; gas 5) for 15 minutes. This will also loosen the skins. Remove from the oven and rub the skins off the peanuts. Grind the peanuts in a food processor.

Put onion in a pan with the oil and cook until it is translucent. Add garlic and chillies. Keep simmering and stir in the water, ground peanuts, cayenne, sugar and salt. When the sauce is smooth, stir in the soy sauce and lemon juice. Keep refrigerated, with a layer of oil on top to seal. It will keep for weeks.

Mefarka

A Jewish cold dish perfumed with mixed spices.

750 g   (1 1/2 lb) lean minced beef
1 kg   (2 lb) fresh broad beans, shelled
2   tablespoons oil
1/2   teaspoon grated nutmeg
1/2   teaspoon whole cloves
1/2   teaspoon ground cinnamon
1/2   teaspoon ground ginger
1/2   teaspoon pepper
1   tablespoon tomato purée
1   teaspoon thyme
3   eggs
1   tablespoon parsley

Steam the broad beans for 10 minutes or until just tender. Heat the oil in a deep pan. Add the minced beef and stir until it is brown. Add the spices and tomato purée, and just enough water to cover. Simmer until the meat is cooked and has absorbed the water. Add the broad beans to the meat and stir. Break the eggs and beat lightly. Pour them into the meat and beans. Stir for a few minutes, then remove from heat. Cool and serve sprinkled with chopped parsley.

Spice Cake

Spice cake keeps well for several weeks in a cake tin.

185 g (6 oz) sultanas
185 ml (6 fl oz) boiling water
155 g (5 oz) dark brown sugar
45 g (1 1/2 oz) butter
250 ml (8 fl oz) buttermilk
2 egg yolks
125 g (4 oz) wholemeal flour
125 g (4 oz) white flour
1 teaspoon bicarbonate of soda
1 teaspoon ground ginger
1 teaspoon ground cinnamon
4 teaspoons ground cloves
2 egg whites, stiffly beaten
Icing sugar (optional)

Soak sultanas in the boiling water. Cream the sugar and butter together. Add the buttermilk and egg yolks to the mixture and beat well.

Sift the flours and spices. Drain the sultanas, dry and coat with flour. Add the flour mixture and sultanas to the moist ingredients and stir well until all the ingredients are well blended.

Fold in the egg whites and pour the mixture into a well greased 20cm x 20cm (8 in.) cake tin. Bake in a preheated oven at 180°C (350°F; gas 4) for 30 minutes. Dust with icing sugar when cool, if liked.

Picnic Fruit Loaf

Your friends will be really impressed if you produce this warm spicy cake at your next picnic. Make the dough before you leave home, of course, and bake it in the ashes of the fire at the picnic. In Australia the mixture is baked in a 'billy can'.

375 g (12 oz) wholemeal flour
125 g (4 oz) bran
1/2 teaspoon salt
1 1/2 teaspoons bicarbonate of soda
3 teaspoons cream of tartar
1 teaspoon French mixed spice (p 44)
1 tablespoon ground cinnamon
2 tablespoons caster sugar
30 g (1 oz) butter
1 tablespoon golden syrup
125 g (4 oz) milk
90 g (3 oz) sultanas
90 g (3 oz) mixed peel

Mix together the flour, bran, salt, soda, cream of tartar, mixed spice, cinnamon and sugar. Rub the butter through with your fingers until the mixture resembles breadcrumbs. Mix the golden syrup with milk and add gradually to the dough. Stir in the sultanas and mixed peel.

Grease a 'billy can' and lightly flour it. Put in the dough, bake in the ashes for 1 1/2 hours. If you cannot obtain a 'billy can', use a loaf tin, tightly wrapped in several layers of foil.

Spicy Tea Blend

This aromatic blend is a refreshing brew for afternoon tea when you need a pick-me-up.

315 g (10 oz) Russian caravan tea-leaves
1/2 cinnamon stick
Dried peel of 1 orange
2 cardamom pods

Mix the ingredients and store in an air-tight container. To make the tea, infuse 1-2 teaspoons in a teapot for 5 minutes and pour.

Spice cake can be eaten as a dessert or as a welcome snack with coffee or a fruit liqueur at the end of the day.

INDEX

Page numbers in **bold** type indicate illustrations.